CLB 847
© 1985 Illustrations: London Features International Ltd., London and
    Gamma, Paris, France.
© 1985 Text: Colour Library Books Ltd., Guildford, Surrey, England.
Display and text filmsetting by Acesetters Ltd., Richmond, Surrey, England.
Produced by AGSA in Barcelona, Spain.
Color separations by Llovet, S.A., Barcelona, Spain.
All rights reserved.
Published 1985 by Crescent Books, distributed by Crown Publishers, Inc.
Printed in Spain.
ISBN 0 517 436159
h g f e d c b a

The BEACH BOYS

by Dean Anthony

CRESCENT BOOKS
NEW YORK

Think of the Beach Boys and you think of girls, sun, sea, sunshine, surf and cars; the good life of teen time California. Think again and the picture becomes blurred, confused. Think of 'Good Vibrations', 'Pet Sounds' and Brian Wilson at the production desk. Think of that grand sound, the kaleidoscopic images. And then hold.

Somewhere between those two images lies the truth: Brian Wilson at the controls, the Beach Boys riding the surf. Complex and simple...

The Beach Boys are an exception in American pop history. For in their music and clothes they came to represent a way of life – a lifestyle. Amongst British groups, with their faddism and cult building, this is more common. In America the Boys were a rarity. A real slice of teen life writ large.

Not only did the Boys represent a lifestyle, they helped to create and recreate that lifestyle for millions of people. Sure, not everybody could sunbathe in California, but with a Beach Boys record playing, it was, to quote the song, 'Fun Fun Fun' all the way.

Their homilies to the good life were gigantic affairs: songs expressing the joys and uncertainties of teen life: candy sweet accompaniments to the beach life.

This is the Beach Boys in their striped shirts on the 'Ed Sullivan' show; the

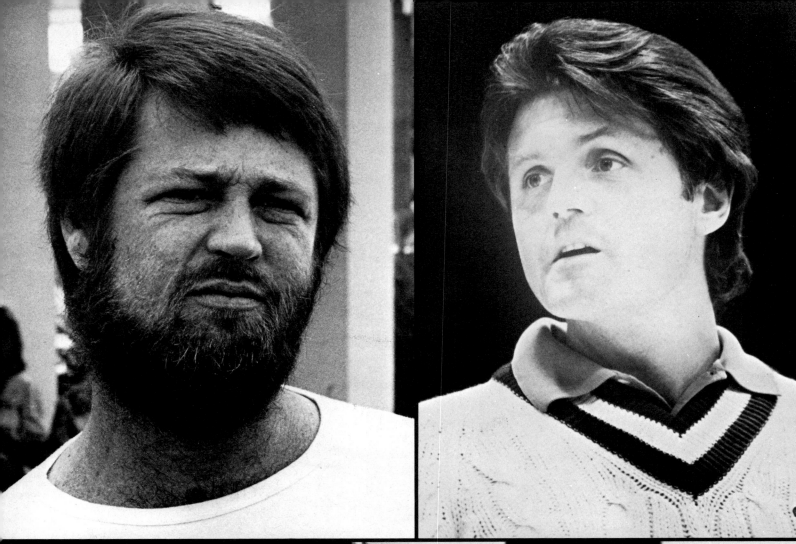

Beach Boys over in England fooling around on 'Ready Steady Go'. The clean cut American guys. The Beach Boys in aspic; forever the sound of summer.

And yet, there was plenty of serious stuff going on here. Its name was Brian Wilson, a musical visionary seeking to expand his art and in doing so pushing his creativity to a near perfect pitch... and then shying away.

Behind the surfin' songs, the goofy teeth photos and all... there was always Brian Wilson; the only threat to the Beatles perpetual hold on mid-Sixties pop aesthetics. Wilson's talent, his use, and perhaps abuse of that talent, his personal obsessions, his unconventional lifestyle... these are perhaps the most important strains running through the Beach Boys' story.

For Brian's progress as a writer/ producer runs side by side with the evolving state of pop itself... his move from Chuck Berry riffs and Four Freshmen style harmonies to complex and restless production masterpieces. These highlighted, indeed at times led, the changing emphasis in Sixties pop. From the simple to the sophisticated.

The Beach Boys as a group traveled that course, indeed survived the rigors of the journey, and moved on. Classic beat pop to giant soundscapes. Opportunistic and innovative. Quite a story...

Hawthorne, California is typical. Typical sunkissed Americana. Wealthy, young and ambitious. Hawthorne is thirty miles from the Pacific Ocean, but three of its inhabitants did more to eulogise that coastline than anybody else. The Wilson family lived in Hawthorne. That's Brian, Dennis and Carl Wilson... the backbone of the Beach Boys.

The Wilsons, like their home town, were seemingly typical. Their father Murray, an ex-songwriter, was a self-made businessman dealing in heavy machinery. Their mother, Audrey, kept house, and the three brothers went to High School. Pretty normal really.

But then there was music. If Murray's forays into songwriting had been unsuccessful he still harbored ambitions in the music biz. So did the Wilsons; albeit of a more innocent manner. Brian, the eldest brother, was the keenest. A conscientious school student, he showed even more ardor for pop music. His favorite band was the Four Freshmen, a close harmony band, clean cut and respectable.

Brian would sit for hours listening to the Freshmens' harmonies and perfecting his own vocal range. All this he tried to tranfer to his own groups. There was Carl and the Passions, Kenny and the Cadets, high school bands playing Brian Wilson's first songs... "My brother Dennis came

home from school one day," remembers Brian, "and he said... 'Listen you guys, it looks like surfin's gonna be the next big craze and... you guys oughta write a song about it'. Cos at that time we were writing songs for friends and school assemblies.

"So it happened we wrote a song just due to Dennis' suggestion, and from there we just got on the surf wagon 'cos we figured it'd be a hot craze. It's all because of my brother though."

Dennis' advice hit pay dirt with 'Surfin', the first single from Brian's new group... the Beach Boys.

The Beach Boys who produced 'Surfin' were: Brian Wilson (bass/keyboards), Carl Wilson (guitar/vocal), Dennis Wilson (drums/vocal), Mike Love, an older cousin (vocal) and David Marks. Marks was quickly replaced by Al Jardin (guitar/vocal) in a Beach Boys line up that, give or take 'live' replacements for Brian, would last.

'Surfin', out on small Los Angeles indie Candix, was a minor hit. The major record companies soon came running. Realizing that the Boys had hit on the mood of the moment, Capitol Records and producer Nik Venet went in for a piece of the action. Represented by Murray Wilson the Beach Boys signed on the dotted line.

Murray was a hard manager. A strict

disciplinarian, he demanded work, work and more work. The Boys duly obliged. Brian's songwriting at the time was prolific: all high harmonies and twangy guitars set to the most perfect teenage lyrics.

Brian Wilson had a genius for keeping in touch with the trends around him. His songs read like a potted history of early Sixties West Coast life: little snapshots of the teen dream. 'Surfin' Safari', 'Surfin' USA', 'Little Deuce Coupe' read like jingles for a new way of life. Young and Californian, they made even the schoolboy from England a proxy member of the American dream.

From almost nothing the Beach Boys concocted a surf music of their own. Set within a loose structure the Boys wedded their clear harmonies and falsetto high

points to a spare soundscape that was the aural equivalent of their windswept lives.

If 'Surfin' U.S.A.', Chuck Berry riffs and all, was the surf anthem of 1962, then Brian's '63 collaboration with Jan Berry of Jan and Dean in the classic 'Surf City' was the sub cult masterpiece. The lyrics spoke of every real beach boy's dream... "two girls for every boy."

Wilson was defining young California. Nothing missed his roving eye. The Beach Boys would ride a trend, look around... and then move on. Brian was quick to pick up on the new craze: motor sports, hot rods.

No sweat, if this was the new thing, then the Beach Boys were going to be the first group to chronicle the new fad on vinyl. The change to motor sports also heralded the first of many changes in

Beach Boys lyric writers. Previously, Brian or vocalist Love had handled the words, now with the exploration of the world of fast cars came one Roger Christian.

Brian takes up the story: "He'd (Christian) get off at midnight, OK, he'd do a night time radio show from 9 to 12 every night and we'd go over to Otto's, order a hot fudge sundae and just whew! talk and talk. We'd be writing lyrics... hustling you know, and all of a sudden we'd realise we'd just written fifteen songs."

Christian's lyrics were pure Americana. Boy meets girl meets souped up motor car. Together, Wilson and Christian created their own picture of teen America. 'Little Deuce Coupe', 'Shut Down', 'Be True To Your School' and 'Spirit of America'. 'Don't Worry Baby' was their tour de force; a seemingly straightforward love story that on closer inspection revolves around lovers' tears over a forthcoming 'chicken run'. In short, all that *angst* is about a piece of motor car devil-may-care... perfect.

t might look like cornball, but really it
s a bit more. The Beach Boys were
ng the ingredients of their
kground and turning them into pure
. If the sentiments were a touch naive,
n it could be said they were only
oing the unbounded optimism of the
ver had it so good' generation.

Of course, Capitol were only too
ling to promote this astute commercial
nt. As the Beach Boys followed the
s so did they; first they issued a
ssary of surfin' terms to DJ's and
ord retailers and now, in 1963, they
e quick off the mark with a dictionary
hot rod terms. The Beach Boys were
tating the commercial odds, not the
ord company. Yet sometimes the pace
uld get just a little too hot. Murray
ked them hard; seven US chart hits in
4, a couple of albums and plenty of
ring. And then some more.

By and large the Boys went for this.
ey enjoyed their success, they liked life
the road. They liked the money. The
ach Boys were the epitome of the life
y sang about. Robust, clean cut and
imistic. That is until December 23,
4.

On that day the pressure finally got to
an Wilson. Traveling on a plane from
s Angeles to Houston for a Beach Boys
ncert he cracked up. This was the first
n that Brian was suffering from
erwork. And not the last. He suffered
similar breakdowns in quick

succession. The king of the teen anthem was going to have to take a rest.

The breakdowns had an immediate effect. Brian stopped touring with the band, to be replaced by a succession of understudies, the most permanent being Bruce Johnstone, the most famous being singer Glenn Campbell.

This was a crucial move for the Beach Boys. For while the Boys were away on tour Brian could get down to the development of his writing/producing talents. Not only did this afford Brian a pleasing concentration on his songwriting, it also gave him time to look around. He began to study the opposition. Principally there was the pure pop talent of the Beatles (they'd knocked the Boys from the top in '64) and the great wall of sound created by one Phil Spector. These were the standards to be beaten.

Meanwhile, the rest of the band was on the road, having fun. More than Brian they were the hot rods of all those songs, good fun-lovin' boys after fame, money and the simple pop formula. They liked it that way. And so, imperceptibly, a fissure opened up between Brian and the band. Only two or so years later would the cracks really begin to appear. But even then it was no shouting match.

So, as the Boys entered 1965, subtle
changes were on the horizon. This was
not immediately noticeable on their next
LP, 'The Beach Boys Today' a careful m[...]
of tried formula, 'Dance, Dance, Dance'
etc and the beginnings of Brian Wilson'[s]
next quantum leap as a producer and
arranger. Just slowly one could begin to
detect something new here, a
strengthening of that sound into
something altogether more kaleidoscopi[c]
  Lyrically the Beach Boys had lost non[e]
of their charm, but bolstering the
sunshine and smiles was a new
worldliness. Things weren't so black an[d]

white anymore. They'd learnt a lot since 'Surfin'' was released in '61; not all of it had come wrapped in teen dream wool either. The Beach Boys were now – well, they were adults.

Brian, for one, was married. He was also, despite the pleading of his songs (after all this was the year of the all-embracing 'California Girls'), getting away from the beach life. Sure, Brian paid homage to teen culture, but his head was somewhere else.

And there was so much to get excited about. In 1965 pop had reached a watershed. If the last two years had seen the emergence of the beat group – simple, effervescent and fun – the next two years were going to be an altogether artier affair. Everything was getting just a bit more serious.

Suddenly Lennon and McCartney were classic composers, Bob Dylan was a poet and the Rolling Stones were the precursors of new attitudes among the young. Compared to Dion it was all pretty heady stuff.

And all the time the stakes were being upped. At the end of the year the Beatles released 'Rubber Soul', the artistic forerunner to 'Revolver' and 'Sgt. Pepper'.

This was pop exploring new ground and Brian Wilson wanted to take the Beach Boys there. He became obsessed, watched their every move and craved the critical plaudits they were afforded.

And yet there were other pressures; commercial pressures for one. Quite simply the Boys had been so successful in forging an identity somewhere between music and image that there was a reluctance to change.

Treading water, they released competent workouts like 'Summer Days (And Summer Nights)' and the camp 'Beach Boys, Beach Party' before Brian Wilson could come to grips with his maturing musical vision. The extension of all that beach mythology over two more

LPs may have been fine for profits but it wasn't going to hasten any artistic breakthroughs.

That would have to wait until 'Pet Sounds' saw the light of day. In retrospect it's possible to see the pointers that pushed Brian Wilson towards this milestone album – retirement from live shows, more time to write, greater awareness of other music – but at the time it was a revelation.

If the elaborate arrangements and haunting moods of 'Pet Sounds' were a surprise to many critics, then the

ophisticated recording techniques were an inspiration to many new groups. The Beach Boys had created an album that put them right at the forefront of the new pop renaissance.

And it all started from such an unpromising base. The Boys were off on tour and Brian had just written two songs for the new LP when Capitol began to panic. It seems the struggle to create the definitive pop of '66 was proving somewhat onerous. Wilson was in trouble and help came from the most unlikely quarter.

"I was really just interested in a regular income," says Tony Asher of his job as a jingle writer. Tony Asher the lyricist on 'Pet Sounds.'

Wilson and Asher had met briefly in the recording studios of LA, where Tony's infatuation with the music biz had led him to hawk his songs. That was it really. Asher was intelligent, sure, but with no training as a songwriter... then wham! he's brought in to collaborate with America's number one pop musician. No logic, just Brian Wilson... and inspired at that.

The recruitment of Asher was crucial to the successful completion of 'Pet Sounds'. Sure, the album's breadth and scope was all Wilson, but Asher's lyrics were a lucid interpretation of Brian's mood. Wilson knew what he wanted for each song, and it was Tony's job to meet the idea with words.

"It's fair to say the general tenor of the lyrics was always his," Asher remembers. "The actual choice of words was usually mine. I was really just his interpreter."

"Even though he was dealing in the most advanced score charts and arrangements," says Asher "he was still incredibly conscious of this commercial thing... this absolute need to relate."

At first it took some time to relate all of this to the rest of the Beach Boys. Frankly, they were a little bit worried

about what Brian and Asher had been up to. The music Brian played to them was, well, a little bit weird. Not the formula they were used to.

There were arguments... but as Brian held most of the artistic trump cards he just had to win.

In a way the Boys had been right, for 'Pet Sounds' was not a great success in the States (it did well in Britain though). Its value has grown as the years have passed.

However, 'Pet Sounds' was a jump up for the Beach Boys. Its appeal relied not on carefully crafted teen anthems, but on a rich, mature composition and on some dazzling studio work. Like Phil Spector, Brian Wilson was now, in his work, openly proclaiming mastery of the studio as an art in itself.

'God Only Knows', 'Wouldn't It Be Nice', 'Caroline No', 'I Just Wasn't Made For These Times' – these were songs to put the Beach Boys' music at the forefront of pop; beautifully arranged and delicately executed.

"I do believe Brian Wilson is a musical genius," says Asher. "Absolutely. Whatever I thought about him personally was almost always overridden by my feelings of awe at what he was creating. I mean he was able to create melodies...

"God only knows where he discovered those chords, those ideas for arranging a certain song..."

In London a grand preview of 'Pet Sounds' at the Hilton had Lennon and McCartney enrapt. The Stones' manager Andrew Loog Oldham declared the record a masterpiece... just the kind of critical acceptance Brian Wilson had sought.

Brian Wilson had a love hate relationship with his work. His plans to record in a gymnasium, his installation of a sand box in the studio were eccentric, sure, but they aimed at one thing – creating the right mood for the Beach Boys' music.

And that mood was most perfectly realized on the Beach Boys hit of autumn '66, the panoramic 'Good Vibrations'. Originally written with Asher, 'Good Vibrations' was re-mixed, re-modeled and re-written with Mike Love after the completion of 'Pet Sounds'. The song is one of the best illustrations of Brian Wilson's obsession with sound, for, according to observers, there are at least 20 versions of 'Good Vibrations' recorded... and rejected as Brian Wilson went for perfection.

He nearly got it as well. Technically superb, 'Good Vibrations' subtle shifts of moods, hypnotic use of the new Moog synthesiser and liquid clarity added up to one blissful state. It was the Beach Boys biggest international hit. Experimentation and commercial success, it seemed like the Beach Boys had hit the right vein.

Yet this did nothing to improve Brian's fluctuating moods. Tony Asher didn't hang around much longer; seeking the security of regular employment he went back to nine to five and left the way open for Brian's next collaborator.

Van Dyke Parks was a complex individual in the LA pop jungle. A former child actor and classical piano student, he'd had a short stint as a would-be soundtrack composer for MGM before drifting into the local pop scene.

"I met him (Brian) during 'Pet Sounds'," remembers Van Dyke Parks. "Brian generously did everything he could to help me along – so I became, as it were, an exercising lyricist. I just started writing the words for him."

It wasn't quite like that. Van Dyke had an enormous impact on Wilson. Intellectual, Van Dyke fulfilled Brian's attempt to make the Boys serious. There were big words in Van Dyke's lyrics, powerful images...

Together, Wilson and Parks launched into a project they believed would even eclipse the artistic achievements of 'Pet Sounds'. Simply entitled 'Smile', that was to be the final proof of the Beach Boys' genius. The blueprints for 'Smile' were put down by Wilson and Parks so that almost a whole album was completed. That album was never released.

15 songs had been completed, a sleeve had been designed. The whole package was ready, top heavy with Van Dyke Parks imagery perhaps, but according to insiders a work of real majesty.

Outside, life went on. The Boys' own label 'Brother Records' was set up: Brian Wilson continued on a whole range of food fads; business meetings were held in the pool; a documentary was made by CBS on Brian and the Beach Boys' new music.

In the middle of all this the 'Smile' project began to fall apart. The rest of the Boys were distinctly fearful of 'Smile's heavy implications on commercial success. Distrusting the wordy Van Dyke,

they reasoned that Brian and his collection of weirdo friends had gone too far this time.

Realising his position between Brian and the band was intolerable, Van Dyke Parks accepted a solo contract from CBS.

Van Dyke gone, the Boys still critical of his work, Brian too began to have his doubts.

Caught between the commercial demands of everyone else and his own self doubt, Brian Wilson caved in. Further intimidated by the release of the Beatles' 'Sgt Pepper' Wilson ditched 'Smile.'

Gone for the moment were 'Cabinessence' 'Surf's Up' et al, though many of 'Smile's' tracks have appeared on subsequent records. A replacement was quickly at hand. Out of the debris of the 'Smile' project and the increasing eccentricity of Brian Wilson's life came 'Smiley Smile.'

'Smiley Smile' was a mix of Wilson-Parks collaborations (notably 'Vegetables' produced by Paul McCartney) and real spook-out stuff... 'She's Goin' Bald', 'Woody Woodpecker Symphony'. In the wake of 'Pet Sounds' and 'Smile' this was certainly a pretty disjointed affair and not

the plateau of creativity Brian Wilson sought.

Still, trauma over, Brian went back to the Boys. His entourage was dismissed for the wholesome pleasures of ten pin bowling and hanging out round the pool. With Mike Love, pragmatic and dependable, taking the role of lyric writer the Beach Boys hit back with a solid, easy album, 'Wild Honey;' nice formula with a hint of Motown.

If the Beach Boys were truly together again, then Brian Wilson's quest for the majestic, the pinnacle of pop, was somewhat denuded. Confidence lost, he continued to provide the Boys with a string of songs, at times brilliant, but often lacking the ambition of his earlier work.

The Beach Boys were going through a tough time. Finding themselves out of place with the California acid rock explosion, they were declared unhip, off the pace and just a little behind the times. The strain began to show in some of the Boys' personal lives. Sure, they still pulled plenty of dollars but...

Dennis Wilson was divorced and disillusioned and finding himself increasingly attracted to the West Coast acid culture. He started divesting himself of his possessions and hanging out with the likes of Charles Manson as his life hit a temporary downward spiral.

And then there was Mike Love's infatuation with transcendental meditation. All the Boys had checked TM, but Mike became really hooked. In May of '68 he came up with the idea of taking the Maharishi Mahesh Yogi on the road with the Boys.

The Boys embarked on a 17 date tour, the second half of each show given over to the noble Maharishi's teaching on 'spiritual regeneration'. Reaction to the tour was so bad that half the dates were cancelled.

Following on from this debacle was
'Friends', the Boys' own half-baked
spirituality mixed with straight pop. It
bombed. The Beach Boys were in a bad
way.

Brian had seemingly opted out of the
fray, writing songs by reflex almost, but
not putting his heart into it. He could,
however, still pull the odd gem from his
Bel-Air mansion. 1969's 'Do It Again' was
a fitting end to a decade as Wilson looked
back to the sun, sea and surf of by gone
days.

It was also the end of a decade as the
Beach Boys quit Capitol for Warners; a
move intended to revive interest in the
band.

Warners were keen to promote the
Boys. Their 'Sunflower' LP of that year –
a classic piece of Beach Boys sweetness –
led to a series of West Coast concerts, an
appearance at the second Monterey
Festival, and critical reassessment. One
concert of this period was not, however, s
rewarding.

And the Beach Boys acquired a new
manager, Jack Riely, and a new direction
Craving the hip credibility that was once
theirs for the asking, they began to play
benefit gigs, talk about political
problems... and released 'Surf's Up' – an

album who's title track was one of the
classics from the discarded 'Smile'
project. The album was a commercial and
critical success, matching choral
harmonies to progressive pop and seeing
the emergence of Carl Wilson from
brother Brian's shadow.

Yet all was not well with the Beach
Boys' new role. To stay with the times
they'd sacrificed some of their pure pop
vision, blurred their unity. With Brian
Wilson increasingly erratic he
contributed just two songs apiece to the
next couple of LPs – 'Carl And The
Passions – So Tough' and 'Holland' –
albums that took a disjointed patchwork
of disparate influences – there was no
leading voice anymore.

And one voice in particular wasn't
going to be around to call the shots. On
June 4, 1973, Murray Wilson died of a
heart attack. Stern disciplinarian or no,
Murray's death had a devastating effect
on the family. Tears were shed... but the
Beach Boys carried on.

Here on in the story becomes a parade of worthy albums, more successful touring, and periodic outbreaks of Beach Boys revivalism. The Boys are still around and making good records, but now they are a legend: a band with a mighty past.

Their work, however, was not the epoch making stuff of the past. '15 Big Ones', 'The Beach Boys Love You', 'M I U Album', 'L A (Light Album)' (an experiment with disco) and 'Keeping The Summer Alive' saw the beach Boys through a decade where their relevance might have decreased but their stature certainly grew. May '75 saw the Boys come from behind to steal a massive Wembley Stadium show from headliner Elton John. 1980 saw them play a benefit concert for Kampuchea, sharing a bill with former rivals Jefferson Starship. In August '83 they were at the center of a row with U.S. Interior Secretary James Watt, who attempted to ban the Boys from playing at the annual Fourth of July celebration in Washington because "rock bands attract the wrong element of people." The Boys were reinstated, much to the relief of fan Vice President George Bush, but declined the offer and instead played before 200,000 devotees on an Atlantic City beach...

There were personal changes, as well. Bruce Johnstone left briefly and came back again. He also wrote 'I Write The Songs' for Barry Manilow. Mike Love, Al Jardine, Carl and Brian presided over the Boys, Brian now the less dominant figure as other talents came forward. In the 'democratization' of the band's creativity some of their unity of vision was lost.

Dennis Wilson contributed to all this, cut one fine solo LP 'Pacific Ocean Blue', appeared in films and then, on December 28, 1983, tragically drowned in the harbor at Marina del Rey. A tragic setting for death seeing that Dennis was a strong swimmer and also the only one of the three Wilson boys who could surf properly. Such is the Beach Boys' standing that condolences were sent from the President on Dennis' tragic death. Dennis was buried at sea, a rare honour for a U.S. civilian...

A sad note to end a story that is built upon the sheer joy and excitement the Beach Boys have given to millions of people. But, they are still around, still one of the quintessential pop groups.

In Spring of '85 U.S. heavy metal vocalist David Lee Roth is high in the U.S. charts with his version of 'California Girls', there are rumours of a new album and perhaps a tour – summer will be with us soon.